**This
Read, Listen, & Wonder
book belongs to:**

_____

_____

_____

CANDLEWICK PRESS

For every blue whale alive today
there were once twenty.
People hunted and killed so many of them
that fewer than 10,000 remain.
Now blue whales are protected
and hunting them is banned,
so in some places their numbers
are growing — very, very slowly.
Still, you could sail the oceans for a year
and never see a single one.

For Joseph and Gabriel
N. D.

For Dilys
N. M.

Text copyright © 1997 by Nicola Davies
Illustrations copyright © 1997 by Nick Maland

First U.S. paperback edition with CD 2008

The Library of Congress has cataloged the hardcover edition as follows:

Davies, Nicola.
Big blue whale / Nicola Davies ; illustrated by Nick Maland.
— 1st U.S. ed.
Summary: Examines the physical characteristics, habits, and habitats
of the blue whale.
ISBN 978-1-56402-895-2 (hardcover)
1. Blue whale — Juvenile literature. [1. Blue whale. 2. Whales.]
I. Maland, Nick, ill. I. Title.
QL737.C424D38 1997
599.5'1 — dc20   96042327

ISBN 978-0-7636-1080-7 (paperback)
ISBN 978-0-7636-3822-1 (paperback with CD)

10 9 8 7 6 5 4 3 2 1

Printed in China

This book was typeset in Centaur.
The illustrations were done in ink and wash.

Candlewick Press
2067 Massachusetts Avenue
Cambridge, Massachusetts 02140

visit us at www.candlewick.com

BIG BLUE
WHALE

Nicola Davies

illustrated by Nick Maland

CANDLEWICK PRESS
CAMBRIDGE, MASSACHUSETTS

The blue whale is big.

Bigger than a giraffe.

Bigger than an elephant.

Bigger than a dinosaur.

The blue whale is
the biggest creature
that has ever lived
on Earth!

Female blue whales are a little bigger than the males.

Blue whales can grow to 100 feet long and weigh 150 tons — that's heavier than 25 elephants or 115 giraffes.

In deep water there isn't much light and it's hard to see. So blue whales use their sense of hearing and their sense of touch to find their way around.

Reach out and touch the blue whale's skin.
It's springy and smooth like a hard-
boiled egg, and it's as slippery
as wet soap.

Look into its eye.
It's as big as a teacup and as dark
as the deep sea. Just behind the eye is a hole
as small as the end of a pencil. The hole is one of
the blue whale's ears — sticking-out ears would
get in the way when the whale is swimming.

9

The blue whale lives all of its long life in the sea.
But it is a mammal like us, and it breathes air, not water.

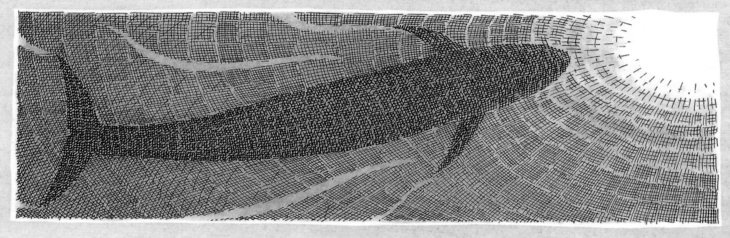

From time to time, it has to come to the surface to breathe
through the blowholes on top of its head.

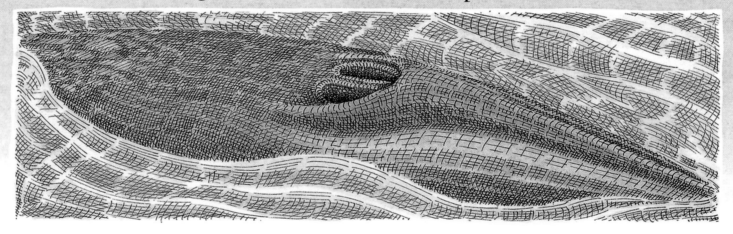

Blue whales can live for about 70 to 80 years.

When it breathes out,
it makes a great misty puff
as high as a house.
This is the whale's blow,
and you can see it from far away.
You can hear it, too — a great

PROOUFF.

And if you are close enough,
you can smell it, as the whale's
breath is stale and fishy!

A blue whale can stay underwater for 30 minutes or more.
But on long journeys, it usually surfaces for air every 2 to 5 minutes.

A blue whale can have
as many as 790 baleen plates in its mouth.
Baleen is tough bendy stuff, like extra-hard fingernails.

Take a look inside its mouth. Don't worry, the blue whale doesn't eat people. It doesn't even have any teeth. It has hundreds of baleen plates, instead. They're the long bristly things hanging down from its top jaw.

The whale doesn't need teeth for biting or chewing, because its food is tiny!

The blue whale
eats krill — pale pinkish
shrimplike creatures the size
of your little finger.

Billions of them live
in the cold seas around
the North and South Poles.
In summer there can be so many
that the water looks pink —
so that's when blue whales
come to the polar seas to eat.
It takes an awful lot of
tiny krill to feed
a great big blue whale.
But the whale doesn't catch
them one at a time.
It has a special way of
swallowing whole swarms
of them at once.

A blue whale can have as many as 88 folds of skin in its throat.

First, it takes a huge gulp of krill and salty seawater.
There's room for all this because the whale's throat unfolds
and opens out like a vast balloon. Then it uses its big tongue
to push the water out between its bristly baleen plates.

The water streams away and leaves the krill caught
on the bristles like peas in a sieve.
Now all the whale has to do is lick them
off and swallow them.

A blue whale can eat about 30 million krill just in one day — that's three big truckloads!

And this is how the blue whale spends the summer —
eating krill and getting fat. But in the fall,
the polar seas freeze over.

In summer, the blue whale grows a thick layer of fat all over its body. This fat is called blubber, and it's a food store for the winter, when the whale eats very little.

The krill hide under the ice where the whale cannot catch them. So the whale swims away from the icy cold and the winter storms.

Day after day, the blue whale swims slowly and steadily toward its winter home. Its huge tail beats up and down to push it along. Its flippers steer it left or right.

For two months and more the whale swims, until at last it reaches the calm warm seas near the equator.

There it stays all winter.

Some blue whales spend their summers around the South Pole and swim north to the equator for the winter.

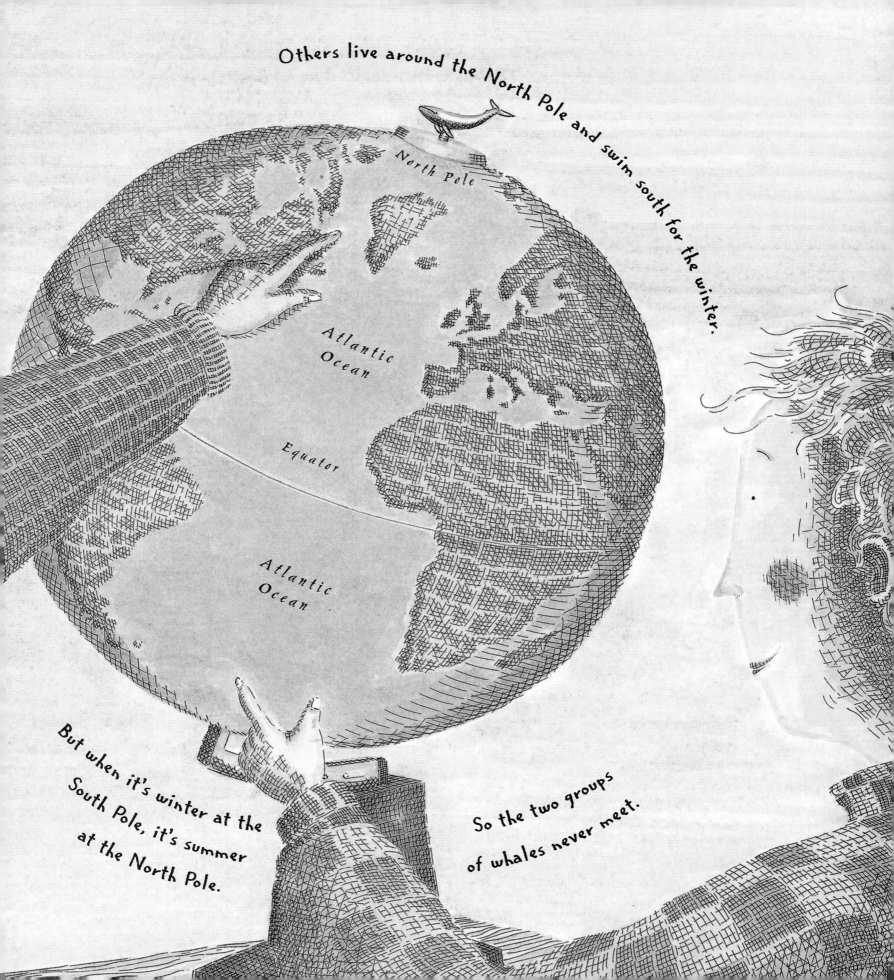

Others live around the North Pole and swim south for the winter.

North Pole

Atlantic Ocean

Equator

Atlantic Ocean

But when it's winter at the South Pole, it's summer at the North Pole.

So the two groups of whales never meet.

And there the blue whale mother gives birth to her baby, where storms and cold weather can't hurt it.

Male and female blue whales mate in winter and then part. Babies are born about a year later.

The blue whale's baby slithers from her body, tail first.
Gently she nudges it to the surface to take its first breath.
Then the baby dives beneath her to take its first drink of milk.

A blue whale baby is 23 feet long at birth. It drinks more than 150 gallons of milk a day, sucking it from the teats tucked into its mother's belly.

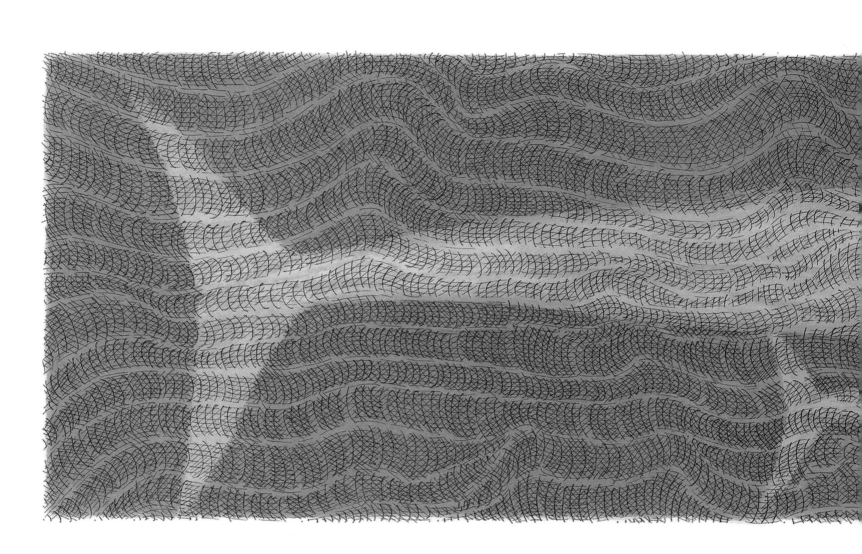

All through the winter, the blue whale keeps
her baby close. It feeds on her creamy milk,
and it grows and grows.
In spring, the two whales return to the polar seas
to feast on krill together. But by the fall,
the young whale is big enough to live on its own.

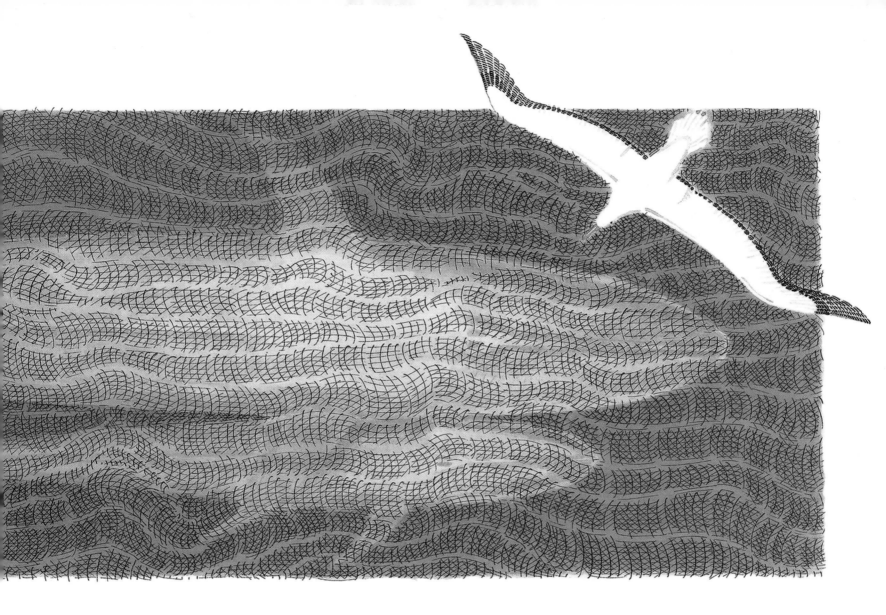

So mother and young whale part and begin
the long journey back to the equator.
A blue whale may travel from the polar seas
to the equator and back every year of its life.
Sometimes it will swim with other blue whales,
but mostly it will swim alone.

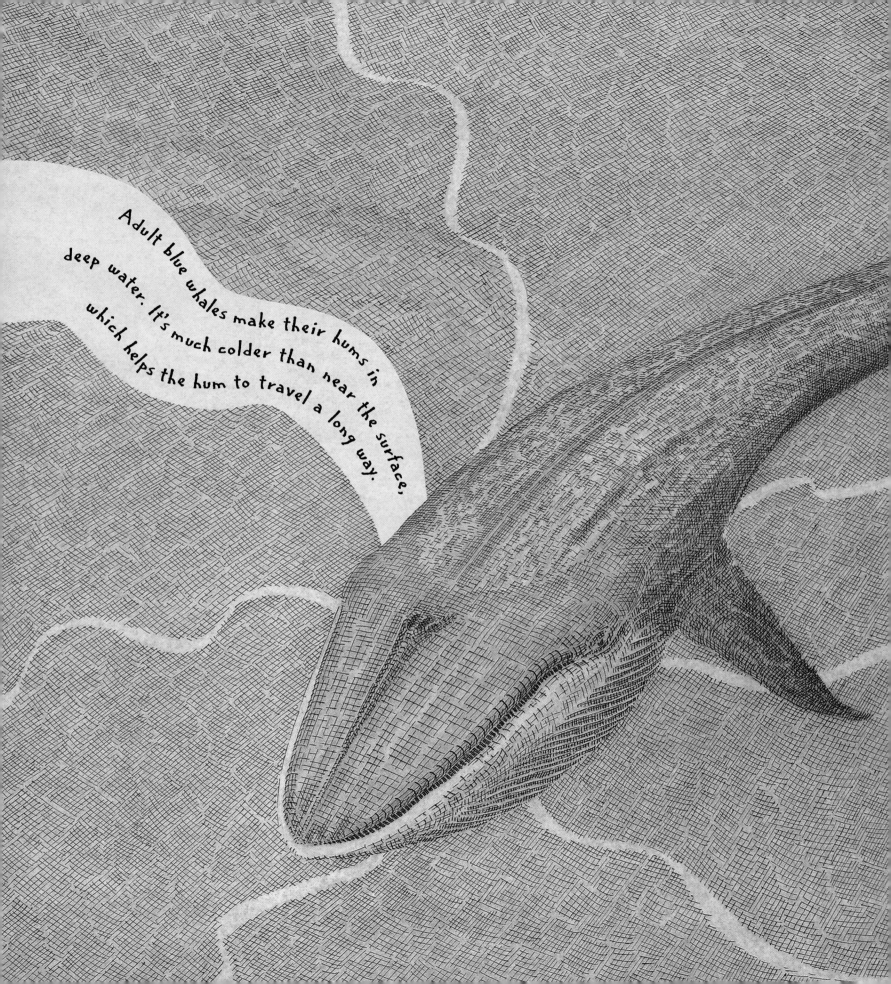

Adult blue whales make their hums in deep water. It's much colder than near the surface, which helps the hum to travel a long way.

Yet, the blue whale may not be
as lonely as it seems.
Because sometimes it makes
a hum — a hum so loud and
so low that it can travel for
thousands of miles through the
seas to reach other blue whales.
Only a very low hum could travel
so far. And only a very big animal
could make a hum so low.
Perhaps that's why blue whales
are the biggest creatures
on Earth — so that they can
talk to one another even when
they are far apart.
Who knows what they say.
"Here I am!" would be enough . . .

because in
the vastness
of the green seas,
even a blue whale is small —
and hard to find.

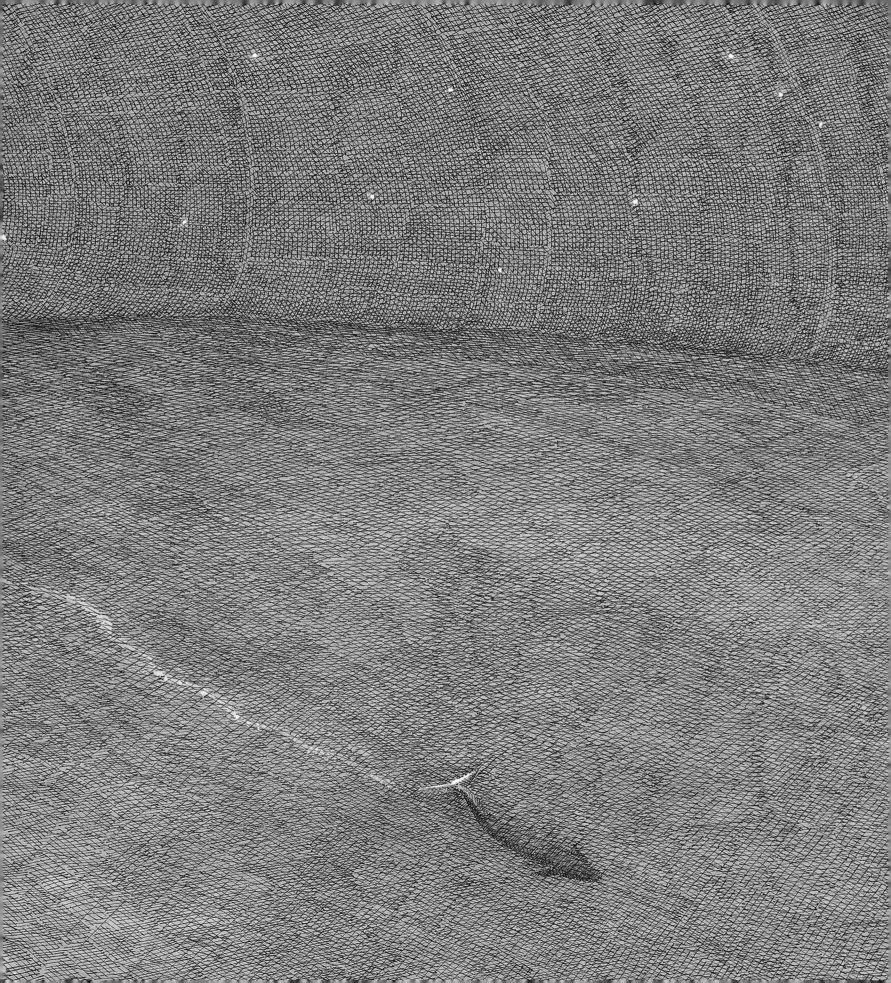

INDEX

Look up the pages to find out about
all these blue whale things.
Don't forget to look at both kinds
of words — this kind *and*
this kind.

NICOLA DAVIES holds a degree in zoology and has studied humpbacks, sperm whales, and blue whales in the open ocean. She says, "Now there is so much man-made noise in the ocean that the blue whales are having trouble hearing one another. Unlike the humpbacks, their booming hums are infrequent, so it is always exciting when we locate one."

NICK MALAND holds degrees in English literature and drama. He began drawing while pursuing a career in acting, and he eventually became a full-time illustrator. "I have illustrated for many newspapers and magazines over the years, but it was not until my daughter, Eloise, was born that I turned to children's books."